DEPORTMENT for DUKES & TIPS for TOFFS

DEPORTMENT for DUKES & TIPS for TOFFS

A Compendium of Useful Information
for Guests at the Mansions of the
Nobility, Gentry, and Clergy

BRUMMELL & BEAU

THE BRITISH LIBRARY

First published in 1900 by Simpkin, Marshall & Co.

This edition published in 2013 by
The British Library
96 Euston Road
London NW1 2DB

British Library Cataloguing in Publication Data
A catalogue record for this publication is available from The British Library

ISBN 978 0 7123 5703 6

Printed in China

CONTENTS

NOTE
TO THOSE INTERESTED IN ART.

THE PLATES accompanying this volume were all originally hand done. With a view to conveying inform-ation as well as pleasure, the non-essential parts of the subjects they illustrate have merely been indicated by a dotted line.

PREFACE.

THE want of a literature appealing only to those moving in the highest social circles, and practically incomprehensible to such as have not enjoyed the same advantages of birth, fortune, and cellars, has long been regretted by the families of the aristocracy, their chaplains, and servants.

To supply it the Authors respectfully beg to offer this treatise. Its ethics are adapted alike to the Throne-room, the boudoir, and the butler's pantry; its style has been carefully moulded on the best traditions of these apartments. During perusal, his Grace (or his valet) will find it applicable to most, if not all, of the contingencies of a ducal existence; after reading, he will be equally delighted with its merits as shaving-paper.

The error into which the caterers for this section of society have hitherto most commonly fallen has been that of dealing with topics also entertaining to the wearers of elastic-sided boots and provincial tailoring. Falling in love, going to sea, and making a fortune are accidents that may befall a policeman; but staying with a Cabinet Minister, taking a Duchess in to dinner, and seeing a cockaded hat touched in deferential recognition, are sensations enjoyed by the favoured few. A visit to a country house (we allude, of course, only to such as possess a practicable back-stairs, and at least two spare bedrooms) is, next to the somewhat rarer experience of wearing a garter, blue ribbon, or other personal marks of Royal favour, the summit of refined gratification.

At the disposal, therefore, of the guest travelling in a reserved carriage towards a twelve-course dinner, the authors have placed their own imaginations and their friends' facts.

The first edition is naturally limited to 10,000 copies.

SOME HINTS ON
THE SELECTION OF INVITATIONS.

1. DISREGARD all unstamped and unsigned invitations to a country house.

2. Give the preference to a week at Margate with a Royal Duke, before two months' deerstalking with a Colonial Bishop.

3. Should, however, your prospective host have, in addition to his ecclesiastical dignities, a Humane Society's Certificate, or an Only Daughter, defer your visit to His Royal Highness till a more convenient date, expressing at the same time your regret at the necessary derangement of his holiday plans.

4. Invitations written on pink paper, all gross mis-

spellings of the invitee's Christian name, and any marked
deviations from the customary methods of address, &c.,
may be answered in the negative by post-card.

'MARGATE,' OR 'ESPLANADE,' OUTFITTING.

5. In answering the invitation you have decided to
accept, a certain familiarity is permitted if your host be
below the rank of life peer; beneath the rank of parish
councillor it is even required

(The following reply of a young gentleman extremely

scrupulous on this point is reproduced by the kind permission of the writer :—

To MRS. CLAUD HOPPER,

Sweed Hall, Neepshire.

DEAR MRS. H.—

I think I remember who you are. Shall come down for the dance if two days' shooting are thrown in. Could also bring a gee and stay for a week if the country is worth it. Wire particulars.

Yours, &c.,

X. Y.

P.S. — Send a covered trap to meet me, and don't keep me waiting at the station)

6. In accepting an invitation from those in the higher social grades, extending from the widows of the tenth sons of barons to members of the Royal House, a slightly different tone is to be adopted. An easy *hauteur* of style, from which anything like false modesty and servility

11

have been rigorously excluded, is a well-recognised sign of *haut ton.*

7. In declining such an invitation, be careful to state the precise grounds of your refusal. (The following is a happy illustration of this maxim :—

MY DEAR DUCHESS,—

I am extremely indebted to you for your invitation, which, however, I regret to say, I cannot accept, as my valet's sister-in-law is at present confined to her room with a slight chill, and my own shooting-boots are being repaired.

Yours, &c.,

A. B.)

8. In accepting a 'dine and sleep' invitation at Windsor, the following hints may be found useful :—

Write both the V. and the R. in capitals, with a full stop after each.

Avoid anything even distantly approaching to a *risqué* allusion or a reference to a contemporary sovereign.

Be careful to convey the impression that you have had some difficulty in extricating yourself from a previous engagement.

Avoid (whenever possible) answering on a post-card.

Inquire particularly whether you are expected to dress

9. In default of a more regular invitation, the following form has been found efficacious in procuring a temporary visit :—

'*To the 4th Beefeater from the end.*

'Shall be under the table at 7 punctually. Whistle "God Save the Queen" if she wears pink shoes, "Rule Britannia" if blue. Keep some dessert. I enclose P.O. for 2s. 6d.'

10. Never decline an invitation too firmly. There are many ups and downs in life.

11. In answering invitations from Hibernian Politicians, Minor Poets, and the Suburbs, it is well to remember that

by opening the ends of the envelope it is sometimes possible to save a halfpenny.

12. A telegram costs sixpence ; there are many acquaintances worth less than that.

PREPARATIONS FOR A VISIT.

1. Never forget that in preparing for a visit, even to a Cabinet Minister, the selection of a suitable wardrobe is a matter of the very first moment.

(The authors are reminded of an instance in which a young man of well-authenticated pedigree and an income of fully a hundred pounds a year lost an extremely good opening as manager of a suburban laundry through omitting to bring a pair of patent leather boots on a visit to a maternal second cousin.)

2. Although the selection of your *belles lettres de train de luxe* may be confidently left to your valet (or valets), attend personally to the packing of your collars : if celluloid, economy of space may be studied by placing them

in your sponge bag; if paper, the lining of your hat may be found more convenient.

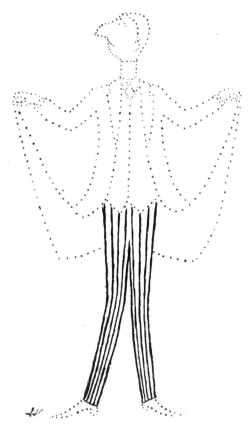

PLEASANT PANTALOONS FOR A YOUNG PEER.

3. In spending a month at an archiepiscopal palace, although sable and gaiters are *de rigueur*, it is nevertheless

16

advisable, in case of tenants' ball or choir practice, to put in a pair of spotted socks . and a practicable shirt-front.

4. The amount of luggage is of importance. While a considerate guest will avoid overwhelming a house-boat during a Saturday to Monday visit with the impedimenta of a touring theatrical company, he will equally observe the inaptitude of starting on a six months' sojourn with an Oriental Monarch equipped merely with a mackintosh and a silk hat.

(The sad fate of the Scotch explorer who recently left for the Arctic Circle in a khaki suit and tennis shoes is a painful illustration of want of thought in this direction.)

5. A hint on the size of luggage may not be without value to the fair sex. It is inadvisable that any trunk should greatly exceed the American standard of 6 ft. by 10 by 7. Comparatively few residences in this

country are provided with sliding roofs and steam-derricks.

The perspicuous Duchess visiting the Dissenting minister will do well to remember the axiom, 'A box in the bedroom is worth six on the lawn.'

THE JOURNEY.

1. Remember that much of the success and comfort of the journey depends upon the impression the traveller produces on his arrival at the railway station.

2. His valet (or valets) should precede him in a cab (or cabs) with the luggage in ample time to secure the undivided services of a large staff of porters, and, if possible, the station-master.

If the traveller be below the rank of Bank Clerk, the latter is essential.

3. One minute before the advertised time of the train's departure the traveller himself should arrive (if in his own carriage it is unnecessary to tip the driver).

19

4. If the train be a few minutes late the time may be profitably occupied by discussing with the station-master the advisability and cost of a special.

It is almost needless to say that this conversation, as indeed his entire conduct, should be loud, authoritative, and overbearing, and should certainly not lack a *soupçon* of gilded arrogance.

5. This *soupçon* should, of course, vary inversely with the traveller's *place de société*. Thus, an Earl may enter the carriage at the wrong side, and retire immediately beneath the seat; while a suburban householder or actor-manager, unless accompanied by a signet-ring bearing his, or its, armorial acquisitions, may not even close the door of the compartment unassisted.

6. Avoid the vulgar and objectionable habit of conversing with your fellow-travellers. Be on your guard when asked a civil question; if you cannot answer rudely, do not reply at all.

7. When disposed for luncheon, communicate with the guard by means of the ingenious apparatus usually supplied

for this purpose. The ensuing stoppage will enable your valet (or valets) to bring the luncheon basket to your compartment without materially disturbing the wine.

EXCLUSIVE ATTITUDE PARTICULARLY RECOMMENDED FOR SUBURBAN
HOUSEHOLDER AND ACTOR MANAGER.

8. If tempted by the length of your journey to alight at a station for refreshments, be sure to see that the knob is pushed well home, and the slot free from adhering particles, before, possibly fruitlessly, inserting your penny.

9. A gentleman in a blue coat and brass buttons will present himself for the first time before the door of your compartment towards the end of your journey, and reiterate a hope that you have travelled in comfort. This is the Guard.

If you happen to be travelling *incognito* he may be personally thanked for his courtesy. If not, he had better be referred to your valet (or valets) for the particulars he requires.

THE ARRIVAL.

1. Dukes, Suffragan-Bishops, and Foreign Ambassadors should alight from the left-hand side of the train. If still in motion, it is perhaps well to use the platform provided for the ordinary passengers.

2. In the event of your not being expected, it is unnecessary to look for your host's carriage at the station.

3. On arriving at his mansion, stop before the front door and ring the bell, which you will perceive at the right-hand side of the entrance.

4. If a Duke, be careful to wipe your boots on the mat provided for this and similar emergencies.

23

5. It is usually superfluous to shake hands with the footman. You will recognise him by the fact of his opening the door.

6. Divest yourself of your ulster and leggings in the porch or vestibule, and place your umbrella in the stand erected for this purpose, leaving the handle uppermost.

7. If on mentioning your name to your host, your appearance should still seem unfamiliar to him, remember to collect these articles again preparatory to your departure.

8. Should you happen, however, to be welcome, mention immediately the probable duration of your visit. It is sometimes exceedingly embarrassing for your host to discover at the end of the fifth week that you propose to depart by an early train on the following morning.

9. Ask your hostess to direct you to your sleeping apartment. Should you find that it is not intended that your valet (or valets) should share this with you, you will then wash your own hands, and afterwards repair to the billiard-room.

10. A dressing - gong will eventually be beaten. **It** is no part of a guest's duties to sound this, but on hearing it you will remove the chalk from your pockets.

AT THE DINNER TABLE.

1. You will probably be directed to take in a young person of the opposite sex to dinner. If an ecclesiastical dignitary or a member of a county family, offer her your right arm, accompanying this gesture with a slight inclination of the head.

2. If, as is quite possible, she accepts your overture, you will then lead her at a moderate pace towards the banqueting apartments.

3. There, if there are chairs enough, you will seat yourself at the table which you will find in the centre of the room.

4. Unfold your serviette. Insert one corner between the back of your collar-stud and the top of your under-vest,

and arrange the rest so that, as far as possible, it may receive the etceteras of your repast.

5. See that your valet (or valets) are stationed immediately behind your own chair, but on no account speak to them until Grace has been said.

HAPPY EXAMPLE OF CLUB AND SOCIETY DINER.

6. If a Bishop, you will say Grace yourself.

7. Do not speak with your mouth quite full; there is a possibility of your being misunderstood. (The authors have

27

known of several unhappy marriages that can only, they think, be attributed to this cause.)

8. The meal concluded, push back your chair, and then, if you are able, rise to your feet.

You will generally find that the ladies leave the room first. Make no audible comment on this. It is a mark of the highest breeding to observe in silence.

AT THE BREAKFAST TABLE.

1. The breakfast table has been aptly described as the gastronomic Scylla, upon which many a social ship has been broken.

(Our readers will doubtless be reminded of the fumigated stockbroker who recently lost a peerage on the very morning of the purchase through being merely two or three hours late for the Prime Ministerial omelette.)

2. It is advisable, therefore (and extremely invigorating), to rise at least four hours before the advertised time for the demolition of this repast. Having shaved, trimmed your nails, and drawn on your slippers (which should be of plain green velvet, adorned merely with

filigree tassels or small pearl buttons), you may proceed to the bath-room.

3. Turn on the tap marked 'Cold' till the receptacle is filled to a depth consistent with safety. Add a pint of hot water and ten drops of eau - de - Cologne ; lather well all over, and then enter the refreshing fluid in person, and disport yourself beneath the surface till clean.

4. You will next attire yourself in your pantaloons (which should be entered feet foremost), complete your toilette by the addition of such refinements of fashion as your taste dictates and your purse affords, and ring for the lift.

5. Should you still have some time on your hands, you will find that the butler's pantry, housekeeper's apartments, and meat safe will amply repay a careful inspection. A genuine interest in these matters is always gratifying to your hostess.

6. In country houses situated beyond the 82° N.

Latitude, it is customary for the guest to appear at breakfast without having effected any material alteration in the costume in which he has spent the night. In England, however, this custom has not yet found general favour; in fact it is advisable to make an almost complete change of attire.

7. A variety of dishes are generally provided for the breakfast table. Among the more common are ham and eggs, buttered eggs, and boiled eggs. Avoid any foolish affectation of ignorance as to their names or ingredients; inquiries on such points will merely prove embarrassing to your hostess and diverting to the servants.

8. Marquesses and their families, guardians, or keepers, now partake of porridge with a spoon. If these are not provided, search may be made for them in the jam-pots and sugar-basins.

9. The programme for the day's amusement will probably be unfolded during breakfast. If a Prime Minister, Provincial Mayor, or foreign Emperor, you will, of

course, have plans of your own, which must on no account be allowed to coincide with those of your host.

10. It is unusual, however, to insist on your personal wishes with more than moderate heat. Anything like an appeal to the fish-forks should, if possible, be avoided.

AMUSEMENTS.

A morning in the country may be very pleasantly spent among the grouse, partridges, foxes, or salmon; or upon the tennis-lawn and cricket-pitch. Equipped with hunting-crop, tennis-ball, and landing-net, the fortunate guest will be in a position to enjoy any or all of these. The following paragraphs, giving more specific directions for excelling in these invigorating pastimes, have been compiled with particular reference to the requirements of the distinguished foreigner.

HUNTING.

1. Hunting is in season (the Bulgarian Count will be interested to learn) throughout the whole year in the British Islands.

This healthy sport falls naturally under three heads— Hunt-the-Fox, Hunt-the-Rat, and Hunt-the-Slipper. It is only right to state, however, that no one can hope to be popularly regarded as an adept in any of these branches unless he be careful to pronounce the word huntin'. (In the latter two branches the gee is, in fact, never used.)

2. The necessary outfit includes a coat of pink (*couleur de rose*) which should button in front, and be long enough to cover the back when the owner (or occupier) is in the saddle ; a black silk or velvet head-piece (*tête-à-tête*) ; and a horse (*de combat*).

3. Some knowledge of the last-named is usually assumed in those participating in this sport. Where this does not exist, the Servian or Siamese tyro is advised to consult the articles to be found in most of the popular encyclopedias under the following headings : ' Girths,' ' Straw-bedding,' ' Bran-mash,' ' Curry-combs.'

Thus prepared, he will be a welcome addition to any hunt.

4. In ordering a mount from a distant mews, it is advisable to state explicitly whether or not you require the services of the driver.

5. A day of Hunt-the-Fox begins with the Meet (*viande fraîche*). Here you will converse with your fellow-sportsmen on the appearance of the dogs and the proposed route. Then follow in the order named the Draw, the Run, and the Brush (no French equivalents), the Bullfinch (*oiseau de bœuf*). the Death of Reynard (*le roi est mort*), and the five-barred gate (*porte de cinq buffet*).

6. Before the meet your mount will be brought to the front door. Should he have been permitted previously

to eat oats or lie down, you may find him fresh (*naïf*). You must then attempt to cajole him towards you by any honourable means within your power; but remember that if the mount will not come to Mahomet, Mahomet must go to the .mount.

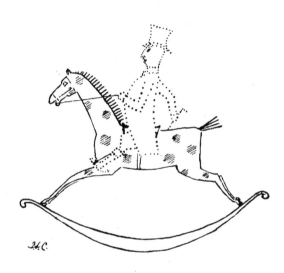

BEST MOUNT FOR HUNTIN' CONVERSATIONALISTS.

7. On your nearer approach the sagacious quadruped will probably turn one of his two ends towards you. That which opens is termed the head; that which wags, the tail.

8. Refrain from pulling yourself up by the last-named. That end does not justify the means.

9. On reaching the top, look for a flat piece of yellow leather. This is the saddle. Seat yourself upon this with your face (if you are right-handed) pointing in the direction in which you expect the animal ultimately to move. Drive your spurs firmly into his flanks (first seeing that the lodge gates are open), and if you are not the first on the field, you will at least have the satisfaction of knowing that your conduct has been characteristic and sportsmanlike.

'TOILETTE À LA CHASSE.'

SHOOTING.

1. For the Shoot (*feu de joie*) there are necessary the quarry, the gun, and the variegated hose. The first is sometimes provided by your host, the others you had better bring yourself.

2. Previous to firing off your fowling-piece (*morceau de poulet*), insert as many cartridges as there happen to be barrels into the end furthest from your destined prey.

3. On sighting the *objet de chasse*, draw the trigger smartly towards you. On again opening your eyes you will thus find that your skill and ardour have sometimes

been rewarded by the decease of the desired animal (*bête noire*).

4. After winging, legging, or otherwise disabling your quarry, the *coup de grâce* is administered. This is entirely an up-and-down stroke, and can be inflicted without unlacing the boot.

5. See that your attendants place the spoil (if of an edible nature, and not entirely dismembered by your attack) in the bags which your host will provide for the purpose. Any possible resuscitation and escape should be guarded against by covering the animal with your musket until life is quite extinct.

6. Never point your gun at your fellow-sportsmen (even in jest) without previously consulting the wishes of your host, and, if he desires it, withdrawing the cartridges.

7. In drawing your gun after you through a hedge, pond, or other hazard, see that the muzzle is directed slightly to one side of you.

(This rule may seem a refinement of precaution, yet at the natural termination of your visit you will have no cause to regret the little extra trouble it has involved.)

OTHER DIVERSIONS.

1. To play the Cricket, bring leg-guards, a spherical leather ball, and a scoring sheet. Write your name on the last-named, leaving a small space for the runs you make. If there are two innings, the result of your efforts is usually termed a Pair of Spectacles.

2. The Golf is an amusing game, but is scored on a different principle. Each stroke is indicated to your opponent by a suitable expletive, and the result is termed a round of the links. In a modified form it may also be enjoyed by ladies.

3. The Fishing needs a worm, a string, patience, and a basket. In the last are placed at the end of the day's enjoyment your flask and waterproof leggings.

4. The Tennis is an active exercise, requiring a pair of white flannel trousers.

IN THE BALL-ROOM.

1. Should you desire to participate in the pleasures of the ball-room, request your hostess or the master of ceremonies to introduce you to one of the young ladies of the party.

2. Mention your name, and apprise her distinctly of the fact that you intend to dance with her before putting your arm around her waist.

3. Clasp her odd hand firmly in yours, and inform the musicians that they may now begin to play.

4. Swing gently to the introductory strains, and then (still adhering to your partner) essay the first step. This should not be too long, and should be made as it were

circularly. The second should follow with the other foot, and this be succeeded by the third and fourth till the middle of the room is reached. By carefully observing these instructions you will find no difficulty in performing most of the simpler evolutions.

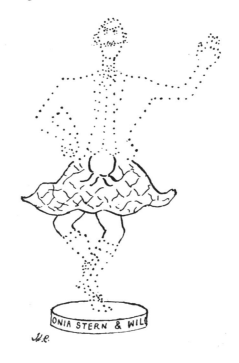

PRIVILEGES ENJOYED BY THOSE OF NORTH BRITISH EXTRACTION.

5. Be particular to stop dancing as soon as the band has ceased playing. This gives your fair partner some

respite, and enables you to prepare yourself for the next measure.

6. Besides revolving with her round the room, you are entitled to further entertain your partner by any or all

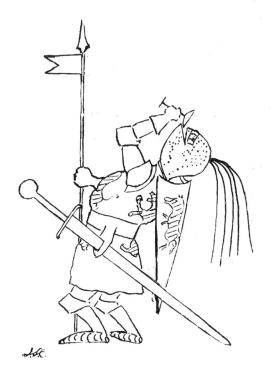

COOL AND CONVENIENT HABIT FOR FANCY-BALL.

of the following devices. You may regale her with soup or sandwiches; you may show her your watch; and you may conduct her through the corridors, conservatories, pantries, and icehouses, or take her to see the children.

7. You must be careful, however, not to adopt the waltzing attitude except when in the act of dancing, and not to enter the private chapel or apartments where invalids are expiring.

8. However warm the evening may be, it is unusual to remove your waistcoat or shirt front.

(The authors are aware that the last temptation is sometimes extremely strong, and a breach of the rule treated leniently in good society. You will find, however, that a bunch of keys or a glass of cold water slipped down the back will be more seemly and equally efficacious.)

THE PRECEDENCE OF PERSONAGES.

Although in the exalted ranks of society to which this volume can only appeal, the question of social precedence has never presented the difficulties with which it is inevitably connected in less fortunate strata, yet the variegated appearance which even the most exclusive boudoir now presents, suggests that the Perplexed Peeress may not find a few hints on this subject superfluous.

1. In the arrangement of a political dinner, charity *soirée*, or other festival more directly devoted to the amusement of the aristocracy, it is necessary for our titled hostess to remember that her guests will approach the provisions with a more equable mind if the formation of attack has been judiciously regulated.

2. Much, of course, depends upon the size of the

party and the number of ices at their disposal. If the former is greatly in excess of the latter, disappointment and dissatisfaction may to some extent be obviated by admitting, in alphabetical order, only those suspected of having previously dined, while such as are of gluttonous habit are distracted by the magic-lantern.

3. Under happier circumstances the following table of precedence, which has been compiled with the assistance of an experienced ex-chamberlain, should be rigorously adhered to. The mastery of its contents will be greatly facilitated, and unseemly friction to a large extent avoided, if copies are framed and hung in conspicuous places in the reception-rooms and corridors.

(Artistic frames suitable for this purpose may be obtained of the publishers.)

A
TABLE OF PRECEDENCE.

---

1. Heirs apparent and their Consorts.
2. Heirs less apparent with their Morganatics.
3. Queens in their own right.
4. Nabobs and their Sultanas.
5. Prime Ministers, Music-hall Stars, and similar dignitaries, with their Ladies.
6. Six-figure incomes.
7. Popes and Black Ambassadors with a selection of their Wives.
8. Poets Laureate (these are invited unaccompanied).
9. White Ambassadors and Eloquent Dissent with whatever they bring.
10. Purifying Influences (we imagine these to be celibate).
11. Gentlemen with evening dress.
12. Gentlemen without.

(Inquiries are never made concerning the *ménage* of the two last classes.)

4. Two Emperors should not sit next one another.

5. We reproduce (with the kind permission of the notabilities concerned) the following correspondence, which happily illustrates the refinements of this subject :—

'DEAR LORDS ⸺ AND ⸺·

'On the last occasion of my entertaining the C⸺ of R⸺, an episode occurred which might have been quite *embarrassing!* The procession having already started for the banqueting apartments, I found that, owing to some slight oversight, I had left upon my hands a Hereditary Elector, the Principal of a Presbyterian Educational Institution, two Ladies-in-waiting, and a Scandinavian Authoress. The question not unnaturally arose, What *was* I to do with them? The Principal could not precede the Elector, nor the Authoress the Ladies-in-waiting; the Principal could not possibly come in contact with the Authoress; while, in *any* case, somebody must be left over!! I should be *so* glad to have your opinion.
'Yours sincerely.'

(Here follows the name of a lady which many would recognise and all respect.)

We admit that the point is a nice one, but we think that this solution (which we despatched by return of post) would meet the emergency.

'Let the Elector take in the two Ladies-in-waiting, the lady who has waited longest being upon the side next the

RECIPE FOR POETS LAUREATE.

balustrade of the staircase. Then let him return for the Authoress. In the meanwhile the Principal should be informed that he has mistaken the house, and that you will be happy to recall his cab'

49

6. The second illustration is as follows :—

' MY DEAR EARLS,—

' I am in *dreadful* trouble, and I know I can rely upon you to help me. We are giving a dinner-party on Friday (our first since Solomon was knighted !), and we have secured such a lot of the *very* smartest people ! ! But there is one thing. Our new marble stairs will hardly be noticed *at all* with all the trains and things, and so Solomon has decided (which I think is a very good idea) to send them down to dinner in single file. This makes a *horrid difficulty*. We have such a *distinguished* guest — the Vice - President of the Dorcas Society. Can he go in just in front of the Consort of a South Pacific Sovereign ? Would the rank matter, or the colours, or anything ? It would suit our *ensemble* so well ! Please give me *full directions*.

' Yours *most* sincerely.'

(This lady, we understand, has substantial claims to notoriety.)

We replied as follows by telegram :—

'Consider experiment risky. Better keep missionary President little further away till Pacific Consort satiated.'

7. We do not think that a more delicate case than these is likely to fall within the experience of our readers.

'CONVERSATION DE SOCIÉTÉ.'

1. The art of *conversation de société* consists in following the obvious to no conclusion.

2. For particular conversations, in any circle of society, the most entertaining subjects are yourself and herself. Punctuate by frequent pauses, and illustrate rather by example than precept.

3. A general conversation in the highest social strata may touch on politics, partridges, and impropriety. In less exalted but still refined circles, on servants, sanitation, and seaside accommodation. The bourgeois may discuss clergymen and internal complaints, and those in humble stations tripe and treason.

4. For practical purposes there are two parts of speech

—the Interjection and the First Personal Pronoun. To these may be added in extremity the Note of Interrogation.

5. The Metaphor, Simile, or Allegory consists in stating what might have been said otherwise a little differently.

6. The Joke, Jest, or Quip is emitted when you are no longer hungry.

To perform one of these, indicate facially that you are about to become humorous, and then say something that is not strictly true about some one smaller than yourself.

(The 'point' is a term once applied to a portion of the joke, jest, or quip. It is now obsolete in good society.)

7. The Repartee is the reply to the joke, jest, or quip. It is most conveniently administered by restating the same in a modified form.

8. When addressed by your own name, reply, 'Here.' When addressed by some one else's, a moment's reflection would convince you that there was some mistake. As

reflection, however, is unfashionable, it is better to reply 'Here' in this case also.

9. Thus begun, your talk is likely to be of at least average interest.

10. If, in the course of your conversation, the rest of the company should happen to quit the room, silence may be practised. This is best learned by endeavouring to think before you speak.

11. The more involved branches of the art of conversation —Telling the Truth, Holding the Tongue, Pulling the Leg, and Sailing close to the Wind—are beyond the scope of an elementary treatise.

THE DEPARTURE.

1. On a hint from your hostess the Departure occurs.

2. This begins by rewarding the servants who have soaped your sponge, blacked your brown boots, or otherwise ministered to your comfort and enjoyment; settling with your host for your washing bill, and informing the Duke, Marquess, or Archbishop who stands next on your list that he may now expect you.

3. We have heard the amount of the reward or tip occasionally discussed. The rule, however, is simple—$1d.$ a day for the butler and upper footmen, $2d.$ a week during a visit of six months or over for the other man-servants, and a shilling left under the mat for the cook.

4. The lady's maid, if pretty, may be rewarded for her services on a separate scale.

5. You next fold your evening trousers, roll up the bed-room clock in the soiled towels, and place these in the bottom

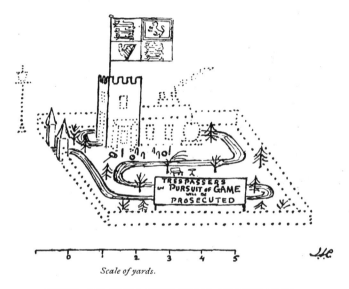

Scale of yards.

DESIGN FOR BIJOU COMBINATION MANSION-VILLA.

of your trunk or band-box. The rest of your packing may be entrusted to your valet (or valets).

6. If still on terms of sufficient familiarity you should then say good-bye to your hostess.

7. To your fellow-guests you may account for the suddenness of your departure by explaining that the telegram from His Royal Highness was peremptory, or that your supply of handkerchiefs is now exhausted.

8. Should they happen to evince regret at your leaving them, you should express your intention of giving them the pleasure of your society at their own mansions or villas at an early, and, if possible, a specified date.

9. The fact of your host remarking 'Thank Heaven!' or 'At last!' when you leave the door may be taken to signify the unqualified success of your visit. You came to enjoy yourself at his expense and you have done it.

10. After departure, it is your duty (and should be your pleasure) to write to your hostess, informing her of your safe arrival at the next Ducal mansion or Archiepiscopal palace, enclosing the foot-bath, photograph frames, or other articles inadvertently packed by your valet (or valets), and expressing your regret for the circumstances that led to the termination of so pleasant a visit.

11. This letter should be brief, worded carefully so as to remove all apprehensions of your immediate return, and may be consigned to the post in the ordinary way (fee up to four ounces, one penny).

THE WHOLE DUTY OF THE GENTLEMAN.

Hitherto this volume has been confined to a consideration of those circumstances in which our well-connected reader is most likely to find himself. We have taken him to the porticoes of the long-descended, the boudoirs of the fashionable, and the coverts of the sportive ; but, just as it is the occasional misfortune of the most tastefully attired to travel in an omnibus (when accompanied by his solicitor, for instance), so it is impossible for even the least un-sophisticated to avoid contingencies unforeseen when he first entered Society. With a few of these we now propose to deal, prefacing our remarks, however, with the warning that, even when not expressly mentioned, we assume the presence of ironed trouserings and a real watch.

1. When a complete change of identity is considered advisable, the acceptance of a Peerage will most effectually, and in the long run most cheaply, accomplish this end.

2. The title chosen should have none but the most cryptogrammic reference to the respectable industry you recently adorned; the fees (we are informed) must be paid in advance, and the editors of *Who's This?* and

ACQUISITION TO THE PEERAGE.

similar compilations should be provided with the particulars of your descent from the historical personage selected.

3. This personage should, if possible, either have been executed for treason, or be a monarch of virile habit. The intervening links should be indicated with extreme brevity.

4. The last point is important. We have heard of
amplified statements being investigated by unscrupulous
persons.

5. A certain degree of latitude is permissible in the size
and colour of the coronet. It should, however, as a rule be
circular, and it will be found more serviceable to have the
interior lined with a non-adhesive waterproofing.

6. Although a convenient headgear for the ordinary
purposes for which peers are employed, it is as well to
remind the conscientious Baron that it need not be worn
on the underground railway, and should never be ironed
against the nap. It is as well to remove it in the bath.

7. Mere Gentlemen range themselves (or are arranged
by their valets) into the following varieties:—Gentlemen by
Birth, Gentlemen by Marriage, and Gentlemen by-and-bye
(or Reservist Gentlemen).

8. Some text-books notice a few other less defined
species (such as Gentlemen of the Press), but we shall
not weary our fastidious reader with details of these.

9. For those falling outside the above classification, the following is an exceedingly important rule to remember, particularly in seasons of national emergency, when classes are apt to be confounded (a most regrettable occurrence).

SPECIAL 'GENTLEMAN' OUTFIT, DESIGNED FOR SUCH AS CAN AFFORD IT.

By paying when you need not, and sufficiently advertising the fact, you may, without any further hesitation, style yourself ' Gentleman.'

10. To the privileged few who have been fortunate enough to secure a copy of this work, we must now say farewell. There are certain matters, it is true, with which we have not yet dealt. The choice of a Club, a Wife, or a Harmonium, together with instructions as to the use of these, and kindred topics, must be left for another occasion ; but our coronets will rest the easier on our brows to think that we have so materially assisted our reader upon his rose- (or strawberry-) leaved path.